For 400 years, Stratford-upon-Avon has been the shrine to [one] man's genius.

William Shakespeare was born here. And, after finding [fame,] fortune and royal favour in London, he died here.

Millions of visitors from all over the world have visited S[tratford] over the centuries. For some it is a pilgrimage, to pay hom[age to] the place which produced England's greatest playwright and poet.

For others, it is a chance to appreciate a town whose past has been so carefully preserved.

Stratford-upon-Avon, and the areas around it, give us vivid insight into the life and time of Shakespeare and his family.

This illustrated guide is designed to highlight the key places of interest.

Seit über 400 Jahren pilgern Besucher in das Städtchen Stratford-upon-Avon, dessen Name unauslöschlich mit dem seines berühmten Sohnes – William Shakespeare – verbunden ist.

In dieser Stadt wurde der geniale Dichter geboren, und hier fand er auch seine letzte Ruhestätte.

Stratford-Upon-Avon und seine Umgebung vermitteln auch heute noch einen lebendigen Eindruck von der Zeit Shakespeares und seiner Familie.

In diesem illustrierten Führer möchten wir Ihnen die wichtigsten Sehenswürdigkeiten vorstellen.

Depuis 400 ans, Stratford-upon-Avon est resté le haut-lieu du génie d'un homme.

William Shakespeare y est né, il y mourut.

Stratford-upon-Avon et ses environs donnent une image très vivante de la vie et de l'époque de Shakespeare et de sa famille.

Ce guide illustré a été conçu pour souligner les lieux qui présentent un intérêt particulier.

In the sixteenth century, **Stratford-upon-Avon** was a thriving commercial community surrounded by rich farmland. Its crafts and markets attracted people from miles around.

The name of the streets which survive today tell not only where business was conducted, but also what was sold: Sheep and Wood Streets (photograph page 2) and Ely (swine) Street for pigs and Rother Street for cattle.

John Shakespeare, was the son of a farmer, decided to seek his fortune in Stratford. He became a trader, specialising in the leather used for glove-making.

With the money he made, he bought half of his lodging house in Henley Street. He also married well. His bride was Mary Arden, who inherited money and farmland at the nearby village of Wilmcote.

In April 1564, Mary and John became the proud parents of a son – William. The exact date of his birth is not known, but the baby was baptised on April 26 at **Holy Trinity Church** (photograph page 3). For the ceremony, the child was carried on the 'finest cushion covered with an embroidered bearing cloth'. The event is recorded in the parish register.

William Shakespeare's birthday is traditionally celebrated on 23 April, which is St George's Day, the patron saint of England. Today it is marked with an important international floral parade through Stratford, attended by people from all over the world. Flags of many nations line the streets as the procession wends its way from Shakespeare's birthplace to his tomb at the church where he was baptised.

The year of his birth was one in which bubonic plague swept through Stratford, as it did the rest of the country. His parents must have been anxious for the welfare of their infant as one in ten of the townsfolk died.

Im sechzehnten Jahrhundert war **Stratford-upon-Avon** eine blühende Handelsgemeinde inmitten fruchtbaren Ackerlands. Handwerk und Märkte zogen Menschen aus der ganzen Umgebung an.

John Shakespeare, der Sohn eines Landwirts, kam nach Stratford, um hier sein Glück zu suchen. Er entschied sich für das Metier des Handschuhmachers.

Das Geschäft florierte, so daß er bald die Hälfte des Hauses kaufen konnte, das er in der Henley Street bewohnte. Auch mit seiner Braut, Mary Arden, machte er eine gute Partie. Sie brachte Geld und Ländereien im nahegelegenen Dörfchen Wilmcote in die Ehe ein.

Im April 1564 konnten Mary und John die Geburt eines Sohnes feiern, dem sie den Namen William gaben. Das genaue Geburtsdatum ist unbekannt. Im Kirchenbuch ist jedoch seine Taufe am 26. April in der Holy Trinity Church von Stratford eingetragen. Das Kind wurde, wie es dort heißt, "auf einem feinen Kissen mit einem gestickten Wickeltuch" zur Taufe getragen.

Der Geburtstag von William Shakespeare wird traditionsgemäß am 23. April gefeiert, am Tag des Hl. Georg, des Schutzpatrons von England. In jüngster Zeit findet an diesem Tag in der Stadt ein prächtiger internationaler Blumenkorso statt, der Besucher aus aller Welt anzieht. Der Zug führt vom Geburtshaus des Dichters durch die mit Fahnen aller Nationen geschmückte Bridge Street bis zu seiner Grabstätte in der Kirche, in der er getauft wurde.

■ Au XVIème siècle, **Stratford-upon-Avon** était une commune au commerce florissant entourée de terres cultivées très riches. Son artisanat et ses marchés attiraient des gens à des kilomètres à la ronde.

John Shakespeare, fils d'un riche propriétaire terrien, décida d'aller faire fortune à Stratford. Il y devint commerçant spécialisé dans le cuir pour la confection des gants.

Avec tout l'argent qu'il gagna, il parvint bientôt à acheter la moitié de la pension de **Henley Street** où il vivait. Sa femme, Mary Arden, hérita de terres, dans le village voisin de Wilmcote, et d'un certain pécule.

En avril 1564, Mary et John devinrent les fiers parents d'un fils, William. On ne connaît pas la date de naissance exacte de ce dernier, mais il fut baptisé le 26 avril en l'église Holy Trinity. Pour la cérémonie, le bébé fut placé sur un "coussin très fin recouvert d'un lange brodé". L'événement figure dans le registre paroissial.

L'anniversaire de William Shakespeare est traditionnellement fêté le 23 avril, le jour de la Saint-George, le saint patron de l'Angleterre. Aujourd'hui, on fête cet anniversaire par un grand défilé floral dans les rues de Stratford que viennent voir des gens du monde entier. A cette occasion, Bridge Street est bordée des drapeaux de tous les pays et la procession, partie du lieu de naissance de Shakespeare, s'achemine jusqu'à la tombe de ce dernier, située en l'église où il fut baptisé.

■ The house in **Henley Street** (*photographs pages 2 & 4*) where William spent his early years is a half-timbered building constructed of local materials: wood from the nearby Forest of Arden and stone from Wilmcote. Immediately above the living room is the room where William was born (*photograph page 6*). Scratched on the window are the signatures of Sir Walter Scott, Thomas Carlyle, Isaac Watts and other visitors – a 'Kilroy-was-here' style of graffiti which records some of the more distinguished tourists of the past.

As young William's father became more prosperous as a businessman, he rose to high position in the town. By 1568, John Shakespeare was High Bailiff (Mayor) of Stratford. With the position came pomp and importance. To functions, fairs or markets he would wear a scarlet fur-trimmed robe and be escorted by uniformed officials carrying maces.

One of his father's civic duties was to license visiting players who wished to entertain in the town. In return, he and his family enjoyed privileged front-row seats to theatrical performances at the **Guildhall**. Young William, aged four, almost certainly watched the actors, who must

have made a powerful impression on him.

The Guildhall, where Shakespeare's father would have attended town council meetings, forms part of Stratford's medieval heritage. The **Guild Chapel** on the corner of Chapel Street dates back to 1269 when leading local figures got together to form the Guild of the Holy Cross, a mutual aid association which became a leading force in the affairs of the town. Traces of medieval wall paintings can still be seen in the Chapel, though the building was altered in the 15th and 16th centuries. The east window shows the history of Stratford.

When aged five, William would probably have been sent to the 'petty' school held in a corner of the old Guild Chapel. There he would have learned the Catechism, and the rudiments of reading, writing and the rigid rules of behaviour. His mother Mary would have been unable to help him with his lessons as she was illiterate. It is recorded that his father John "affixed his mark" to official papers, so, like his wife, he was probably also unable to read or write.

◼ Das Fachwerkhaus in der **Henley Street** (Foto S. 4), in dem William seine frühe Kindheit verbrachte, ist ganz aus einheimischem Material gebaut: Holz aus dem nahen Forest of Arden und Stein aus Wilmcote. Heute ist es als Shakespeare-Gedächtnismuseum eingerichtet. Unmittelbar über dem Wohnraum kann man das Zimmer besichtigen, in dem William Shakespeare geboren wurde (Foto S. 6).

Mit dem geschäftlichen Erfolg von John Shakespeare stieg auch sein Ansehen in der Stadt. 1568 hatte er es zum High Bailiff, d.h. Bürgermeister, von Stratford gebracht.

Zu seinen Amtspflichten gehörte es unter anderem, fahrenden Schauspielertruppen die Genehmigung zu erteilen, in der Stadt aufzutreten. Die Familie Shakespeare hatte also bei den Vostellungen in der Guildhall zweifellos immer die besten Plätze. Auf den kleinen William, der zu dieser Zeit etwa vier Jahre alt war, dürften die Schauspieler einen starken Eindruck gemacht haben.

Die mittelalterliche Guildhall an der Ecke von Chapel Lane, in der Shakespeares Vater an den Sitzungen des Stadtrats teilnahm, geht bis auf das Jahr 1269 zurück. Damals gründeten führende Persönlichkeiten des Ortes die "Guild of the Holy Cross", eine Vereinigung zur gegenseitigen Unterstützung, die sich zu einer wichtigen Kraft im Leben der Stadt entwickelte. Die Kapelle wurde im 15. und 16. Jahrhundert baulich verändert, Reste mittelalterlicher Wandgemälde blieben jedoch erhalten.

Im Alter von fünf Jahren kam William Shakespeare wahrscheinlich in die Kinderschule ("petty school"), wo Katechismus, Lesen und Schreiben und vor allem gutes Benehmen und Disziplin auf dem Lehrplan standen.

◼ Le maison de **Henley Street** (Photo page 4) où le petit William passa ses premières années est une maison à colombage construite avec les matériaux de la région: du bois de la forêt voisine d'Arden et des pierres de Wilmcote. La pièce où naquit William est située juste au-dessus de la salle de séjour. (Photo page 6)

Commerçant devenu homme d'affaires très prospère, le père de William accéda dans sa commune à une éminente fonction. En 1568, John Shakespeare devint en effet bailli (maire) de Stratford.

L'un de ses devoirs civiques consistait à délivrer des autorisations aux acteurs qui voulaient monter des divertissements dans la commune. En retour, lui et sa famille avaient le privilège d'occuper les sièges du premier rang lors des représentations théâtrales données au **Guildhall**. Il est pratiquement certain que le jeune William, qui avait alors quatre ans, eut l'occasion de voir jouer des acteurs, lesquels durent lui faire une impression très marquante.

Le Guildhall (palais des corporations-hôtel de ville), où le père de Shakespeare aurait participé aux réunions du conseil municipal, fait partie de l'héritage médiéval de Stratford. La chapelle du cercle paroissial (Guild Chapel), au coin de Chapel Lane, date de 1269, époque à laquelle les notables de la ville s'y rassemblaient pour former la corporation de la Sainte Croix, une association d'entraide qui exerça une puissante influence sur les affaires de la ville. On peut encore voir des traces de peintures murales dans la chapelle, bien que l'édifice fut modifié aux XVème et XVIème siècles.

Lorsque William eut cinq ans, son père l'aurait envoyé à l'école primaire située au coin de la vieille "Guild Chapel". Il y aurait appris le catéchisme, les rudiments de la lecture et de l'écriture et les règles très strictes de la bonne conduite.

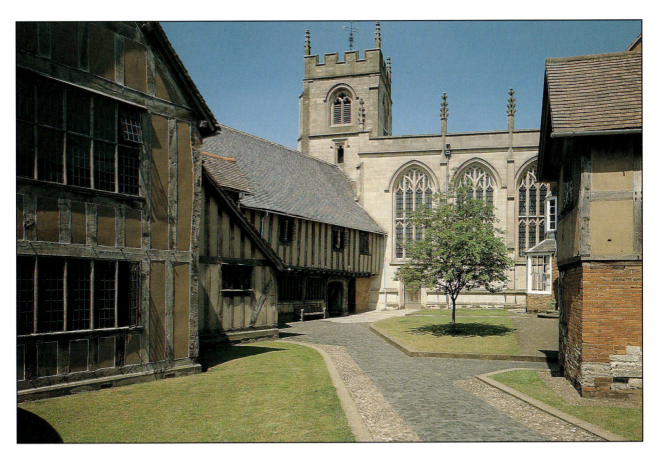

■ At the age of 7, William would have been ready to attend the free **Grammar School** *(photographs pages 7 & 8)*. The single schoolroom above the Guildhall is still used today.

In William's time, it had a good educational reputation but the regime was long and harsh. In summer, lessons, which were all conducted in Latin, started at 6am (7am in winter) and would last eleven hours a day, six days a week, with holidays of two weeks at Christmas and two at Easter. One schoolmaster of the time is recorded as whipping the boys in winter simply to warm himself up. In his later plays, Shakespeare's references to school were always cynical.

When William was about 11 years old, Queen Elizabeth visited the Earl of Leicester at **Kenilworth Castle** *(photograph page 8)*. The Queen's royal progress around England drew sightseers from all over the area to marvel at the colourful court processions and the stunning entertainments that were staged over three weeks for the royal guest. Kenilworth had been a royal residence from the 12th century onwards. Though now in ruins, its' massive central keep had walls over 20 feet thick at the base. The Earl of Leicester built the gatehouse and other additions to the castle, including a pleasure garden. Shakespeare might well have been among the spectators to have seen plays performed here.

William's father, meanwhile, had ambitious ideas of his own. He applied at the Herald's College for the coat of arms of a gentleman. He was turned down.

His business then also suffered a downturn. Young William left school early – at the age of thirteen – as he was needed to help revive the family fortunes. It is likely that he assisted his father in the leather trade.

■ *Mit sieben Jahren wechselte er dann vermutlich in die* **Grammar School***, die Lateinschule, über (Foto S. 7). Das Klassenzimmer über der Guildhall wird heute noch benutzt.*

William war ungefähr elf Jahre alt, als Königin Elisabeth I. den Grafen von Leicester in **Kenilworth Castle** *(Foto S. 8) besuchte. Viele Schaulustige aus der ganzen Gegend fanden sich ein, um den prunkvollen, farbenprächtigen Zug der Königin und ihres Hofstaates zu bewundern und die aufregenden Veranstaltungen mitzuerleben, die drei Wochen lang zur Unterhaltung der Monarchin und ihres Gefolges stattfanden. Kenilworth, von dem heute nur noch eine Ruine steht, war seit dem 12. Jahrhundert eine königliche Residenz. In der Mitte ragte eine massive Festung auf, deren Wände unten eine Dicke von mehr als 20 Metern erreichten. Der Earl of Leicester fügte ein Wachhaus und andere Anlagen hinzu, darunter auch einen Garten. Shakespeare könnte sehr wohl unter den Zuschauern bei den Theateraufführungen gewesen sein.*

Shakespeares Vater fehlte es nicht an ehrgeizigen Ideen. So bewarb er sich beim Herald's College um das Wappen eines Gentleman. Sein Antrag wurde abgelehnt.

Danach ging es mit Geschäft von Shakespeare Senior bergab. Der junge William verließ vorzeitig – mit dreizehn Jahren – die Schule, wahrscheinlich, um seinem Vater im Ledergeschäft zu helfen.

■ *A sept ans, William aurait été prêt pour entrer au collège communal, gratuit (Photo page 7). L'unique salle de classe,* située au-dessus du Guildhall, est encore utilisée aujourd'hui.

L'année où William atteint ses onze ans, la Reine Elizabeth vint rendre visite au Comte de Leicester, au **château de Kenilworth** (Photo page 8). Les déplacements de la Reine dans tout le pays attiraient des badauds de toutes les régions qui venaient s'émerveiller devant la procession de la cour et les divertissements sensationnels que l'on organisait pendant trois semaines pour les dignitaires du royaume. Bien qu'aujourd'hui en ruine, le château de Kenilworth, avec son imposant donjon et ses murailles de plus de 6 mètres d'épaisseur à la base, devint une résidence royale à partir du XIIème. Le Comte de Leicester fit contruire le corps-de-garde et apporta d'autres compléments au château, dont un jardin d'agrément.

Là encore, il se peut fort bien que Shakespeare fît partie des spectateurs qui y virent jouer des pièces de théâtre.

Le père de William, pendant ce temps, nourrissait certaines ambitions. Il demanda au Herald's College de lui attribuer les armoiries d'un gentilhomme. Mais elles lui furent refusées.

Ses activités commencèrent alors à accuser une nette récession. Le jeune William quitta l'école très tôt (à treize ans) car la famille 8avait besoin du lui pour l'aider à redresser ses revers de fortune. Il est probable qu'il assista alors son père dans son commerce du cuir.

The Guild Chapel, the Grammar School & Almshouses, Church Street.

■ Then, at the age of 18, William Shakespeare found love. By the summer of 1582, he was courting 26-year-old Anne Hathaway, who came from a prosperous family at Shottery. The house, now known as **Anne Hathaway's Cottage** (*photographs pages 9 & 10*), is a mile across the fields from Henley Street. The thatched farmhouse stayed in the Hathaway family for a further three centuries and some of the furniture which can be seen today belonged to Anne's descendants.

William and Anne were hastily married by special licence as she was pregnant. She brought to the marriage a dowry of £6. 13s 4d (£6.66p.) and the newlyweds moved into the Shakespeare family home in Henley Street. In May 1583 Anne gave birth to a daughter, Susanna. Twins Hamnet and Judith were born two years later.

There followed seven 'lost years' when there is no record of William's activities. All that is known is that by 1592, he is first recorded as a writer and actor in London.

Jahre später wurden Zwillinge, Hamnet und Judith, geboren.

Hieran schließen sich sieben "verlorene Jahre" an, in denen Shakespeare nach London gelangt sein muß, für die es jedoch keinerlei verläßliche Spuren gibt. Als nächstes wird 1592 erstmals seine Verbindung zum Londoner Theater erwähnt. Spätestens 1594 gehörte er als Schauspieler, Stückeschreiber und Teilhaber einer Theatertruppe an.

■ *Puis, à l'âge de dix-huit ans, William Shakespeare rencontra l'amour. A l'été 1582, il courtisa une jeune fille de 26 ans, Anne Hathaway, issue d'une riche famille de Shottery. La maison des Hathaway connue aujourd'hui sous le nom de* **Anne Hathaway's Cottage** *(Photos page 9) est située à 1,5 km de Henley Street à travers champs. Cette ferme au toit de chaume resta dans la famille Hathaway pendant encore trois siècles. La plupart des meubles que l'on peut y voir aujourd'hui appartenaient aux descendants d'Anne Hathaway.*

William et Anne se marièrent en hâte et par autorisation spéciale car Anne était enceinte. Les jeunes mariés s'installèrent dans la maison familiale des Shakespeare de Henley Street. En 1583, Anne donna naissance à une fille, Susanna, et deux ans plus tard à des jumeaux, Hammet et Judith.

Puis sept "années oubliées" s'ensuivirent dont on ne sait rien sur les activités de Shakespeare. On ne retrouve sa trace qu'en 1592, alors qu'il est installé à Londres où il travaille comme auteur et acteur.

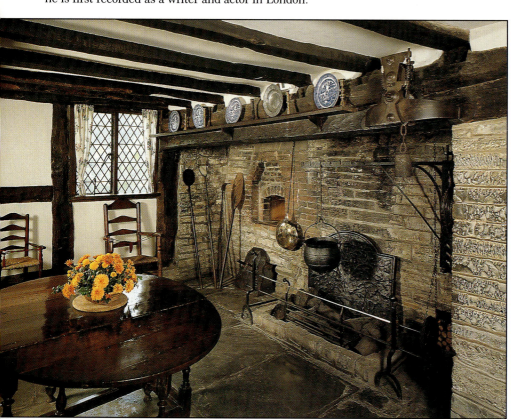

■ *Mit achtzehn Jahren, im Sommer 1582, warb Shakespeare um die Gunst der acht Jahre älteren Anne Hathaway. Anne stammte aus einer wohlhabenden Landwirtsfamilie im nahen Shottery. Das heute als* **Anne Hathaway Cottage** *(Foto S. 9) bekannte Haus seiner Schwiegereltern ist querfeldein rund anderthalb Kilometer von Henley Street entfernt. Das strohgedeckte Farmhaus blieb weitere dreihundert Jahre im Besitz der Familie Hathaway. Die meisten Möbel, die heute hier stehen, gehörten Anne Hathaways Nachfahren.*

Da Anne ein Kind erwartete, wurde das Paar eilig mit einer Sondergenehmigung getraut.

Die Jungvermählten zogen in Shakespeares Vaterhaus in der Henley Street. Im Mai 1583 brachte Anne eine Tochter, Susanna, zur Welt. Zwei

■ There is a tale that he was caught poaching deer at **Charlecote Park** (*photograph page 11*), four miles from Stratford. The owner was Sir Thomas Lucy, who two years earlier had put one of William Shakespeare's relatives (Edward Arden on his mother's side) to the gallows. The story is certainly plausible, as the incident would have provided skins for the family business, meat for the cook-pot – and would also have gone some way to avenge his relative's fatal sentence.

Charlecote House, an Elizabethan mansion still set in its graceful parkland stocked with deer, is now owned by the National Trust and illustrates the lifestyle of a leading country gentleman and his family.

Some say William Shakespeare was forced to leave Stratford because of the disgrace the 'unlawful hunting' charge had brought his father, a chief alderman of the town. Others feel that the reason he deserted his young family was because the lure of the theatre had become irresistible. Shakespeare was 23 – and the arts were flourishing in the glorious and glittering reign of Queen Elizabeth I.

This decisive year for Shakespeare – 1592 – was also noted for the plague which wiped out 11,500 Londoners. Preachers blamed plays for the plague and theatres were closed for two years. Shakespeare switched to poems for which he became famous.

For writing a play, he would be paid up to £10. His words came swiftly and accurately "with scarce a blot in his papers" according to his admiring fellow actors. He carefully invested his earnings and according to one chronicler visited his wife and children back at Stratford once a year.

By 1596 his talent was widely hailed. But when he returned home to Stratford it was for a sad reason – the funeral of his son, Hamnet, who died aged 11. While in his home town, William paid off his father's debts which were so bad that "he dare not go into church for a year" for fear of meeting his creditors. With family honour repaid, when the Shakespeares reapplied for a Coat of Arms it was granted. It bears the motto: Non sanz droict – not without right.

■ *Eine nicht belegte Geschichte besagt, daß man Shakespeare beim Wildern im rund 6 km von Stratford entfernten* **Charlecote Park** *(Foto S. 11) erwischte. Der Eigentümer, Sir Thomas Lucy, hatte zwei Jahre zuvor einen Verwandten mütterlicherseits von William Shakespeare, Edward Arden, an den Galgen gebracht. Die Wilderergeschichte erscheint plausibel, da ein derartiges Unternehmen nicht nur Häute für das Geschäft und Fleisch für den Kochtopf der Familie Shakespeare bedeutet hätte, sondern auch eine gewisse Rache für den Tod seines Verwandten.*

Einige vermuten, daß Shakespeare Stratford verlassen mußte, nachdem er durch diese "ungesetzliche Jagd" Schande über seinen Vater gebracht hatte, der schließlich im Stadtrat saß.

Andere sind der Ansicht, daß er seine Familie verließ, um dem unwiderstehlichen Ruf des Theaters zu folgen. Shakespeare war inzwischen 23 Jahre alt – und die Künste erlebten unter der glorreichen Herrschaft von Elisabeth I. eine glanzvolle Blütezeit.

Das entscheidende Jahr für Shakespeare – 1592 – ging auch durch eine große Pestepedemie in die Geschichte ein, der 11500 Einwohner von London zum Opfer fielen. Puritanische Prediger sahen sie Wurzel des Übels in den Theateraufführungen, woraufhin die Schauspielhäuser zwei Jahre lang geschlossen blieben. Shakespeare wandte sich Sonetten zu, mit denen er sich bald als genialer Lyriker profilierte.

1596 war er als Dichter und Stückeschreiber bereits weitverbreitet geschätzt. Seine Rückkehr nach Stratford war jedoch ein trauriger Anlaß – das Begräbnis seines Sohnes Hamnet, der mit nur 11 Jahren gestorben war. Shakespeares Vater war zunehmend in Schulden geraten, die inzwischen so hoch waren, daß "er sich ein Jahr lang nicht in die Kirche wagte", aus Furcht, seinen Gläubigern zu begegnen. William tilgte die Schulden. Damit war die Ehre der Familie wiederhergestellt. Man beantragte erneut ein Familienwappen, und diesmal wurde es auch genehmigt. Es trägt den Wahlspruch: "Non sanz droict" – nicht ohne Recht.

■ *On raconte qu'il fut pris en train de chasser le cerf sans autorisation dans* **Charlecote Park** *(Photo page 11), à six kilomètres de Stratford. Le propriétaire des terres était alors Sir Thomas Lucy, celui-là même qui deux ans auparavant avait envoyé l'un des parents de William Shakespeare (Edward Arden, du côté de sa mère) à la potence. L'histoire est certes plausible, car le produit de la chasse aurait fourni des peaux pour l'entreprise familiale, de la viande dans sa marmite et aurait été une façon pour William Shakespeare de venger la sentance qui fut prononcée contre son parent.*

Certains disent qui Shakespeare fut obligé de quitter Stratford à cause du déshonneur que l'épisode de la chasse illégale avait infligé à son père, alors magistrat municipal. D'autres pensent qu'il déserta sa petite famille parce que l'attrait du théâtre lui était devenu irrésistible. Shakespeare avait alors 23 ans et les arts florissaient sous le règne brillant et glorieux de la Reine Elizabeth I.

Cette année 1592, décisive pour Shakespeare, resta aussi dans les annales car la peste emporta 11 500 Londoniens. Les prêtres attaquèrent le théâtre, qu'ils rendaient responsables du fléau et les établissements furent fermés pendant deux ans. Pendant cette période, Shakespeare écrivit des poèmes qui le firent connaître.

En 1596, son talent était très largement salué. Mais ce fut pour une triste raison qu'il rentra chez lui: les funérailles de son fils Hamnet, décédé à l'âge de 11 ans. Pendant son séjour dans sa ville natale, Shakespeare paya les dettes de son père, des dettes si lourdes que pendant un an ce dernier "n'avait pas osé se rendre à l'église" de peur de rencontrer ses créanciers. L'honneur de la famille rétabli, les Shakespeare refirent une demande d'armoiries qui fut acceptée. L'écusson porte la mention : Non sanz droict.

■ Das Stadtgespräch in Stratford zu jener Zeit war der Bau eine großartigen, dreistöckigen Hauses,, **Harvard House** (Foto S. 12) in der Hauptstraße, an der Stelle eines alten Gebäudes, das einem Brand zum Opfer gefallen war.

Im folgenden Jahr erwarb William Shakespeare für £ 60 das Anwesen New Place in der Nähe der Guild Chapel, das als das schönste Haus in Stratford galt. Es heißt, daß Shakespeare im Garten des Hauses, in dem er seinen Ruhestand verbringen wollte, eigenhändig einen Maulbeerbaum pflanzte.

■ A ce moment-là, à Stratford, l'attention était concentrée sur la construction d'une maison à trois étages au style très orné: **Harvard House** (Photo page 12), dans High Street, qui vint remplacer une maison détruite dans un incendie.

L'année suivante, Shakespeare investit 60 £ dans une propriété. Il acheta "New Place", une maison que l'on disait la plus belle de Stratford, près de la Guild Chapel. L'auteur dramatique aurait planté un mûrier dans le jardin de la maison qu'il aurait achetée pour ses vieux jours.

Detail of houses in the High Street.

■ The news in Stratford at the time was of the building of an ornate three-storied house, **Harvard House** (*photograph page* 12) in High Street, which replaced one destroyed in a fire. It was built by Thomas Rogers, an alderman of the town. His daughter Katherine was the mother of John Harvard who founded the American University.

The following year, Shakespeare invested £60 in property. He bought **New Place**, said to be the finest house in Stratford, near the Guild Chapel. The playwright is said to have planted a mulberry tree in the garden of the house that he earmarked for his retirement.

But he was not yet ready to lay down his pen. By 1603 a new King was about to be crowned. James I enjoyed the theatre even more than Queen Elizabeth before him. Yet plays were still regarded as somewhat risque entertainments and had to be licensed before they could be performed. A Clerk of the Revels, responsible for licensing, misspelt the Bard's name as Shaxberd.

■ Back home in Stratford, Shakespeare's daughters were preparing to leave the family home. His elder daughter Susanna married a local doctor, John Hall in 1607. **Hall's Croft** (*photograph page 14*) is a stylish half-timbered gabled house where they lived. The dispensary (*photograph page 14*) is complete with drug jars, herbs and the medical equipment the good doctor might have used. A preparation for the plague called for the feathers to be pulled from the tail of a live pullet "and apply him to the sore – the pullet will gape and labour for life and in the end will die." The dose was to be repeated until either the pullets stopped dying – or the patient did. One of the delights of Hall's Croft house is its large walled garden which evokes the plants and trees, flowers and shrubs of Tudor time.

■ *Shakespeares Töchter waren inzwischen erwachsen. Die ältere, Susanna, heiratete 1607 einen einheimischen Arzt, John Hall. Sie wohnten in Hall's Croft (Foto S. 14), einem eleganten Fachwerkhaus mit Giebeldach. In der Apotheke (Foto S. 14) sind Pillenflaschen, Kräuter und Instrumente zu sehen, wie sie zur Ausrüstung eines guten Arztes von damals gehörten.*

Eine wahre Augenweide ist der große, von einer Mauer umgebene Garten von Hall's Croft mit für die Tudorzeit charakteristischen Bäumen, Blumen und Büschen.

■ *Les filles de Shakespeare se préparaient alors à quitter le toit familial. En 1607 sa fille aînée, Susanna, épousa un docteur, John Hall. Ils vécurent à* **Hall's Croft** *(Photos pages 14) dans une maison à colombage et à pignons très élégante. On peut voir aujourd'hui, exposées dans l'oficine de la maison (Photo page 13), les pots de breuvages, les herbes et le matériel médical tels que les aurait utilisés le docteur.*

Délice de cette maison, le grand jardin clos renferme des plantes, des arbres, des fleurs et des arbustes de l'époque des Tudors.

■ In 1611, Shakespeare left London life behind him and returned to his home town. By then, he had a grandchild, Elizabeth, born to Susanna and John. His younger daughter, Judith, married Thomas Quiney, a wine-shop keeper. The house on the corner of High Street and Bridge Street, is Thomas Quiney's old home.

Quiney's father Richard had once written to Shakespeare begging for a £30 loan to pay all the debts he owed in London. The letter – to his 'loving good friend and countryman, Mr Wm. Shakespeare' was never sent and survives as the only letter written to Shakespeare that still exists. It is one of the treasures of the **Shakespeare Centre** *(photograph page 16)* which occupies a site overlooking the garden of the great man's birthplace in Henley Street.

Shakespeare's friend, playwright Ben Jonson, visited him in Stratford in April 1616. They "had a merry meeting and, it seems, drank too hard; for Shakespeare died of a fever there contracted". He died on his birthday, aged 52, and his body was buried in the chancel of **Holy Trinity Church,** *(photograph page 17)* where his monument may be seen. The gravestone bears the inscription:

Good frend for Jesus sake forebeare
To digg the dust encloased heare;

Blese be ye man yt spares thes stones
And curst be he yt moves my bones.

The memorial bust in Holy Trinity Church, ordered by Shakespeare's family from a stonemason who lived near the Globe Theatre in London, is said to be a very good likeness.

But what of the man himself? He appears to have been easy-going, kind and good humoured according to those who knew him. Ben Jonson, a contemporary playwright described his friend in glowing terms: "He was indeed honest and of an open and free nature; had an excellent fancy (imagination), brave notions and gentle expression…"

John Aubrey the antiquarian, described Shakespeare as "a handsome, well shaped man, very good company" and with a "very ready and pleasant smooth wit".

Nicholas Rowe, Shakespeare's first biographer, spoke of the Bard as a "good natured man, of great sweetness in his manners and a most agreeable companion."

In his will, Shakespeare left £10 to the poor of Stratford, and to his wife Anne he left "my second-best bed". Daughter Susanna received the bulk of the estate. His legacy to the world was the unrivalled collection of plays and sonnets.

■ *1611 verließ Shakespeare London und kehrte ganz nach Stratford zurück. Zu dieser Zeit hatte er bereits ein Enkelkind, Elisabeth, die Tochter von Susanna und John Hall. Seine jüngere Tochter, Judith, heiratete Thomas Quyney, einen Weinhändler. Im Haus von Thomas Quyney an der Ecke High Street und Bridge Street.*

Quyneys Vater, Richard, hatte einst einen Brief an Shakespeare verfaßt, in dem er diesen um ein Darlehen von £ 30 Pfund zur Tilgung seiner Schulden in London bat. Der an seinen "lieben, guten Freund und Landsmann, Herrn Wm. Shakespeare" adressierte Brief wurde nie abgeschickt und ist der einzige Brief an Shakespeare, der noch existiert. Heute gehört er zu den Schätzen des **Shakespeare Centre** *(Foto S. 16), von dem man einen Blick auf den Garten des Shakespeare-Geburtshauses in der Henley Street hat.*

Im April 1616 besuchte Shakespeares Freund, der

Schriftsteller Ben Jonson, den Dichter in Stratford. Sie "feierten und tranken, wie es schien, zu viel; denn Shakespeare starb an einem Fieber, das er sich dazumal zuzog". Er starb an seinem 52. Geburtstag und wurde in der **Holy Trinity Church** (Foto S. 17) begraben. Das Grabmal trägt die Inschrift:

Good frend for Jesus sake forbeare
To digg the dust encloased heare;
Blese be ye man yt spares thes stones
And curst be he yt moves my bones.

Sie ist eine einfache Bitte, den Frieden des Dahingegangenen und seine sterblichen Überreste nicht zu stören.

Die büste in der Holy Trinity Church wurde von der Familie Shakespeares bei einem Steinmetz in der Nähe des Globe-Theaters in London in Auftrag gegeben und soll ein authentisches Bildnis des großen Dichters sein.

In seinem Testament hinterließ Shakespeare den Armen von Stratford £ 10 und seiner Frau Anne "sein zweitbestes Bett". Der Großteil der Erbschaft ging an die Tochter Susanna. Der Welt hinterließ er ein kostbares, unvergängliches Erbe in Form seiner Dramen und Sonette.

■ En 1611, Shakespeare quitta Londres pour revenir vivre dans sa ville natale. Il avait alors une petite-fille, Elizabeth, fille de Susanna et de John. Sa fille cadette, Judith, épousa Thomas Quiney, un marchand de vins. L'ancienne maison de ce dernier, située au coin de High Street et de Bridge Street.

Le père de Quyney, Richard, écrivit un jour à Shakespeare pour le prier de lui prêter les 30 £ qui lui permettraient de rembourser toutes les dettes qu'il avait accumulées à Londres. Cette lettre, "à son bon ami et gentleman Mr Wm Shakespeare" ne fut jamais envoyée. Elle reste aujourd'hui la seule lettre encore existante qui ait été écrite à Shakespeare. Elle constitue l'un des trésors du **Shakespeare Centre** (Photo page 16) qui surplombe le jardin du lieu de naissance du grand homme, dans Henley Street.

Le dramaturge Ben Jonson, ami de Shakespeare, lui rendit visite à Stratford en avril 1616. "Très heureux de se revoir, il semble qu'ils burent démesurément, car Shakespeare mourut des fièvres qu'il contracta à cette occasion". Il mourut le jour de son anniversaire, à l'âge de 52 ans. Sa dépouille fut enterrée dans le choeur de l'église **Holy Trinity** (Photos pages 17), où l'on peut voir aujourd'hui le monument érigé à sa mémoire. La pierre tombale porte l'inscription:

Good friend for Jesus sake forbeare
To digg the dust encloased heare;
Blese be ye man yt spares thes stones
And curst be he yt moves my bones.

(Ami, pour l'amour de Dieu
Ne retire pas la poussière que renferme ce lieu,
Béni soit celui qui épargnera ce tombeau
Et maudit soit celui qui en déplacera les os.)

Le buste de Shakespeare que l'on peut voir dans Holy Trinity Church et qui fut commandé par la famille de Shakespeare à un tailleur de pierres qui vivait près du théâtre du Globe, à Londres, serait paraît-il très ressemblant.

Dans son testament, Shakespeare laissa 10 £ aux pauvres de Stratford et, à sa femme Anne laissa son "deuxième meilleur lit"; à sa fille Susanna il donna la plus grosse partie de l'héritage, et au monde, il légua une collection inégalée de pièces et de sonnets.

■ Seven years after his death, his friends published the First Folio of 1623 – a complete edition of his histories, comedies and tragedies. By 1643, Queen Henrietta Maria, wife of Charles I, visited the town as a guest of Shakespeare's daughter Susanna at **New Place**. Only the site and the foundations remain now. The entrance to the gardens in which the foundations are preserved is entered through **Nash's House** (now a local history museum) *(photograph page 18)*. The house *(photograph page 19)* belonged to Thomas Nash, who married Shakespeare's grand - daughter Elizabeth.

■ *Sieben Jahre nach Shakespeares Tod im Jahre 1623 brachten zwei seiner Schauspielerkollegen die "Erste Folio-Ausgabe" seiner Werke heraus, in der zum erstenmal sämtliche Geschichtsdramen, Komödien und Tragödien vereint waren. 1643 weilte Königin Henrietta Maria, die Gemahlin von Charles I, als Gast von Shakespeares Tochter Susanna in **New Place**. Von diesem Haus haben nur die Grundmauern überdauert. Den Garten, in dem sie zu besichtigen sind, betritt man durch **Nash House** (Foto S. 18). Der einstige Besitzer, Thomas Nash, heiratete Shakespeares Enkelin Elisabeth. Heute ist das Haus als Heimatmuseum eingerichtet.* (Foto S. 19)

■ Sept ans après sa mort, en 1623, ses amis publièrent un premier folio: une édition complète de ses histoires, ses comédies et ses tragédies. En 1643, la Reine Henrietta Maria, femme de Charles I, se rendit à Stratford, invitée à **New Place** par la fille de Shakespeare, Susanna. Aujourd'hui, seuls restent de cette propriété le site et les fondations. L'entrée des jardins où sont conservées les fondations est maintenant située à la **Nash's House** (Photo page 18), qui est aujourd'hui un musée d'histoire régionale. La maison appartenait à Thomas Nash, qui épousa la petite-fille de Shakespeare, Elizabeth (Photo Page 19).

■ Alongside the foundations of New Place is the **Great Garden**. It contains cut box and yew hedges. Although close to the bustling heart of Stratford, the Great Garden is a tranquil and quiet spot.

During the 17th century Stratford became widely recognised for the genius it nurtured. But notoriety was also visited upon the town. The Gunpowder Plot conspirators met at Clopton House. After the Civil War's Battle of Edgehill, plundering Royalists and Parliamentarians in turn made heavy demands on the townsfolk's patience and hospitality.

By the 18th century, Stratford's Shakespeare industry was given a boost by the famous actor David Garrick who organised a three-day Shakespeare festival. He also dedicated the new **Town Hall** to the memory of the great man. A statue of Shakespeare can be seen on the **Sheep Street** side of the building.

Shakespeare memorabilia was the rage of the 19th century. Visitors to the Bard's home town were shown fake personal relics which they were assured once belonged to Shakespeare himself.

The **Knott Garden** (*photograph page 20*) by the foundations is a replica of the intricately interlaced and colourful Elizabethan garden designs. The garden is divided by paths into four 'knotts' or beds.

Not even the mulberry tree said to have been planted by Shakespeare in the grounds of New Place remains. It was cut down in the 18th century by a clergyman who was annoyed by the constant stream of sightseers. He later quarrelled with the town authorities, and had the house itself demolished.

■ *Der Knott Garden (Foto S. 20) neben den Grundmauern des historischen Hauses ist einem elisabethanischen Garten nachempfunden, mit farbenprächtigen, kompliziert verschlungenen Mustern. Durch die Wege wird er in vier "knotts" (Rabatten) unterteilt.*

*Auch der angeblich von Shakespeare selbst im Garten von **New Place** gepflanzte Maulbeerbaum steht nicht mehr. Er wurde im 18. Jahrhundert von einem Pfarrer gefällt, der sich über den ständigen Strom von Besuchern ärgerte.*

*An die Überreste von New Place schließt sich der **Great Garden** (Foto S. 20) an. Mit seinen gestutzten Buchsbaum – und Eibenhecken ist er eine Oase der Ruhe und des Friedens mitten im geschäftigen Zentrum der Stadt.*

Im 17. Jahrhundert breitete sich der Ruf Stratfords als Heimatstadt Shakespeares weiter aus. Aber auch berüchtigte Gestalten verbanden sich mit dem Namen der Stadt. So trafen sich zum Beispiel die Verschwörer des berühmten "Gunpowder Plot", die unter ihrem Anführer Guy Fawkes das Parlamentsgebäude in die Luft jagen wollten, hier in Clopton House.

Im 18. Jahrhundert erlebte die Shakespeare-"Industrie" in Stratford einen großen Aufschwung. Der berühmte Schauspieler David Garrick veranstaltete dreitägige Shakespeare/Festspiele und weihte das neue Rathaus ein, das dem Gedenken des großen Dichters gewidmet wurde. An der der Sheep Street zugewandten Seite des Rathauses steht ein Shakespeare-Denkmal.

Shakespeare-Gedenkstücke waren im 19. Jahrhundert große Mode. Stratford-Besuchern wurden häufig gefälschte Gegenstände präsentiert, die – wie man ihnen versicherte – Shakespeare persönlich gehört hatten.

■ *Le Knott Garden, près des fondations, est une réplique des jardins Elizabéthains à entrecroisements très complexes et très colorés. Le jardin est divisé en quatre "bouquets" ou parterres.*

Il n'y reste pas même le mûrier que Shakespeare aurait planté à New Place. L'arbre fut abattu au XVIIIème siècle par un ecclésiastique que le flux continu des curieux incommodait.

*Le long des fondations de **New Place**, on peut voir le **Great Garden** (Photo page 20). Ce jardin est bordé de haies d'if et de buis. Bien que très proche du centre de Stratford, très animé, le Great Garden est un endroit tranquille et très calme.*

Au XVIIème siècle, la ville de Stratford devint très connue pour le génie qu'elle avait engendré. Mais elle eut aussi une triste réputation: les conspirateurs du Gunpowder Plot se réunissaient en effet à Clopton House.

*Au XVIIIème siècle, l'industrie de Stratford prit un second souffle grâce au célèbre acteur David Garrick, qui organisa un festival Shakespeare de trois jours. Cet acteur dédia également le nouvel **hôtel de ville** à la mémoire du grand écrivain. On peut voir une statue de Shakespeare sur la façade du bâtiment donnant sur Sheep Street.*

Le souvenir de Shakespeare fit fureur pendant tout le XIXème siècle. On montrait à l'époque aux visiteurs qui se rendaient dans la ville natale du "chantre d'Avon" des reliques personnelles qui, leur assurait-on, avaient appartenu à Shakespeare lui-même.

■ To prevent such rip-offs, the Shakespeare Birthplace Trust was set up and in 1847 bought the Bard's birthplace to be preserved as a national memorial. The Trust has since acquired the main buildings associated with Shakespeare and his family. Each year they are visited by more than a million visitors, most of whom come from abroad. The Trust's headquarters is the Shakespeare Centre in Henley Street, built from contributions from Shakespeare lovers all over the world to commemorate the 400th anniversary of his birth in 1964.

But the most fitting memorial to his genius are the plays which have been performed every year without fail for over a century. The Stratford Festival is held in the last two weeks of July and as well as musical and theatrical events, it includes a colourful **carnival** (*photograph page 21*).

■ Um derartige Betrügereien zu verhindern, wurde der "Shakespeare Birthplace Trust" gegründet. 1847 kaufte der Trust das Geburtshaus des Dichters, um es als historische Gedächtnisstätte zu bewahren. Seither hat der Trust die wichtigsten mit Shakespeare und seiner Familie verbundenen Gebäude erworben. Jahr für Jahr kommen über eine Million Besucher nach Stratford-upon-Avon, die meisten davon aus dem Ausland. Die Zentrale des Trust befindet sich im Shakespeare Centre in der Henley Street. Das durch Spenden von Shakespeare-Freunden aus aller Welt finanzierte Gedächtniszentrum wurde 1964 anläßlich des 400. Geburtstages von Shakespeare eröffnet.

Die beste Huldigung des großen Genies Shakespeares sind jedoch wohl die seit über einem Jahrhundert veranstalteten Stratforder Festspiele, bei denen alljährlich seine Werke aufgeführt werden. Die zweiwöchigen Festspiele im Juli bieten neben Theater und Musikveranstaltungen einen farbenprächtigen Umzug (Foto S. 21).

■ Pour prévenir de telles "escroqueries", on fonda le Shakespeare Birthplace Trust qui, en 1847, racheta le lieu de naissance de l'auteur afin qu'il soit conservé comme monument commémoratif national. Depuis, le "Trust" a également acheté les principaux bâtiments associés à Shakespeare et à sa famille. Chaque année plus d'un million de personnes, le plus souvent venues de l'étranger, viennent les visiter. Le Siège du Trust se situe au Shakespeare Centre, dans Henley Street. Ce centre fut construit en 1964 grâce aux contributions faites par des admirateurs de Shakespeare du monde entier pour commémorer le 400ème anniversaire de sa naissance.

Mais les souvenirs qui rappellent le mieux son génie restent sans conteste toutes le pièces qui ont été jouées chaque année sans exception et depuis plus d'un siècle dans le cadre du festifal de Stratford. Cette manifestation se déroule pendant les deux dernières semaines de juillet. En plus des représentations théâtrales et musicales, elle s'accompagne aussi d'un carnaval très coloré. (Photo page 21).

■ **The Royal Shakespeare Theatre** is a controversial example of early 1930s architecture. The red-brick bulky building by the **River Avon** (*photograph page 22*) was the winning design in a competition for a replacement for an earlier theatre which burned down.

The river today is one of the delights of Stratford. Leisure boats meander lazily to and fro and green fringes of gardens provide a calm backdrop to Stratford's cultural and historic gems. But wherever you go in Stratford you are rarely far from a reminder of the town's most famous son. The **Shakespeare Statue** (Gower Memorial) in the Bancroft Gardens was presented to the town in 1888. The playwright is seated on a stone plinth. Around him are characters from his plays – Hamlet, Lady Macbeth, Falstaff and Prince Hal (*photograph page 22*).

The Shakespeare connection stretches farther than the town's immediate boundaries. Mary Arden's house (*photograph page 24*) at **Wilmcote**, just over three miles from Stratford, is the home of the poet's mother. A Tudor farmhouse, it is built of oak beams from the nearby Forest of Arden and local Wilmcote stone. Its interior gives a fascinating glimpse of the plain rustic charm of a typical Warwickshire farmstead's kitchen, hall, dairy and living rooms. Its homespun collection of farm implements and domestic equipment and furniture now form a rural life museum.

■ Das Royal Shakespeare Theatre ist ein umstrittenes Beispiel für die Architektur der frühen 30er Jahre. Der massive rote Ziegelbau am River Avon (Foto S. 22) erhielt den ersten Preis bei einem Wettbewerb für ein neues Shakespeare-Gedächtnistheater, nachdem das alte durch einen Brand zerstört wurde.

In Stratford gibt es kaum einen Ort, an dem man nicht an den großen Sohn der Stadt erinnert wird. Das **Shakespeare-Denkmal** (Gower Memorial) in den Bancroft Gardens (Foto S. 24) wurde der Stadt 1888 gestiftet. Der Dichter sitzt auf einem Steinsockel, umgeben von Figuren aus seinen Stücken – Hamlet, Lady Macbeth, Falstaff und Prinz Hal.

Die Shakespeare-Assoziationen gehen über die Stadt hinaus. In Wilmcote, gute vier Kilometer von Stratford, steht das Haus von Shakespeare's Mutter, Mary Arden (Foto S. 24). Das Tudor-Farmhaus ist mit Eichenbalken aus dem nahen Forest of Arden und Stein aus Wilmcote gebaut. Sein Inneres vermittelt einen guten Eindruck vom rustikalen Charm eines typischen Warkwickshire-Farmhauses mit Molkereiräumen, Küche, Vorraum und Wohnbereich.

Aerial photograph of centre of Stratford showing the Royal Shakespeare Theatre, New Place and the Guild Chapel.

■ Le Royal Shakespeare Theatre est un exemple très controversé de l'architecture du début des années trente. Ce bâtiment très imposant, de construction récente et situé en bordure de la rivière Avon (Photo page 22), est le résultat du concours qui fut organisé pour remplacer un ancien théâtre qui avait brûlé.

Où que vous alliez dans Stratford, vous verrez toujours quelque chose qui évoquera le souvenir du personnage le plus célèbre qu'ait jamais enfanté la ville. La **Statue de Shakespeare** (Gower Memorial) (Photo page 22), exposée dans les jardins de Bancroft, fut donnée à la ville en 1888. Elle représente le dramaturge assis sur un socle en pierre, entouré des personnages de ses pièces: Hamlet, Lady Macbeth, Falstaff et le Prince Hal.

La lignée des Shakespeare s'étend bien au-delà des limites immédiates de la ville. La maison de Mary Arden (Photo page 24), à Wilmcote, à cinq kilomètres de Stratford, fut la demeure de la mère du poète. Cette maison de ferme de l'époque des Tudors est faite en poutres en chênes taillées dans le bois de la forêt voisine d'Arden et en pierre de Wilmcote. Son intérieur donne un aperçu fascinant du charme rustique très simple d'une cuisine, d'une entrée, d'une laiterie et d'une salle de séjour d'une ferme typique du Warwickshire.

AROUND AND ABOUT STRATFORD-UPON-AVON

The Warwickshire countryside around Stratford-upon-Avon is known as Shakespeare country... "that shire which we the heart of England well may call". The landscape, traditional buildings and historical and literary roots of the area together form an important and picturesque part of the English heritage.

The village of **Bidford - on - Avon** is where William Shakespeare is reputed to have suffered a serious hangover after revels at The Falcon public house. The village has become a modest mecca in recent years for the revival of Morris dancing. The Shakespeare **Morris Men** (*photograph page 26*) of Stratford-upon-Avon have made a special study of Bidford's traditional dances, which they have revived. Morris dancing itself is an ancient ritual which goes back over a thousand years. The particular style performed in the Cotswolds area is considered true Morris.

The Forest of Arden is an ancient woodland area where Shakespeare set much of his play As You Like It. His mother's name was Arden. **Henley-in-Arden** village on the main Stratford road (*photograph page 26*) is studded with tipsy half-timbered buildings. Its features include the earthworks of a Norman stronghold and the Beaudesert Church with Norman architecture.

Baddesley Clinton village's fame partly arises from the deeds of one of its Lords of the Manor. Nicholas Brome murdered the local rector who had tickled Brome's wife under the chin. When he died in 1517, Brome asked to be buried where everyone would tread on his grave as his penance. Visitors to Baddesley Clinton church step on his stone as they cross the threshold. A more traditional memorial to him is featured in the east window, where he is pictured kneeling in prayer.

His family home, Baddesley Clinton Manor, (*photograph page 27*) is a unique example of a late medieval moated manor house. It was owned by the Ferrers family for nearly 500 years until taken over by the National Trust.

DIE UMGEBUNG VON STRATFORD-UPON-AVON

Die Grafschaft Warwick rund um Stratford ist als "Shakespeare Country", d.h. das Land Shakespeares, bekannt . . . "die Grafschaft, die wir wohl das Herz von England nennen dürfen". Die Landschaft, die alten Bauwerke und die historischen und literarischen Wurzeln dieser Gegend verkörpern einen bedeutenden, pittoresken Teil englischer Tradition.

Im Dorf **Bidford-on-Avon** soll William Shakespeare im Gasthof zum Falken zu kräftig dem Alkohol zugesprochen und sich einen schweren Kopf geholt haben. In jüngster Zeit hat sich der Ort zu einem Zentrum für Anhänger des traditionellen Morris-Tanzes entwickelt. Die **Shakespeare Morris Men** (Foto S. 26) von Stratford-upon-Avon haben die Tradition dieses über tausend Jahre alten Tanzes in Bidford studiert und wiederbelebt.

Der Forest of Arden ist ein altes Waldgebiet, den Shakespeare unter anderem als Kulisse für sein Stück "Wie es Euch gefällt" wählte. Der Name von Shakespeares Mutter war Arden. Im Dörfchen **Henley-in-Arden** an der Hauptstraße nach Stratford finden sich viele malerische, bucklige Fachwerkhäuschen (Foto S. 26).

Das Dorf **Baddesley Clinton** ist für die Missetat eines seiner Gutsherren, eines gewissen Nicholas Brome, bekannt. Brome ermordete den Rektor des Orts. Das Opfer hatte sich nichts anderes zu Schulden kommen lassen, als die Frau des Gutsherren am Kinn zu kitzeln.

Das Haus des Nicholas Brome, Baddesley Clinton Manor (Foto S. 27), ist ein ausgezeichnetes Beispiel für einen spätmittelalterlichen Herrensitz mit Wassergraben.

LA CAMPAGNE AUTOUR DE STRATFORD-UPON-AVON

La campagne du Warwickshire, autour de Stratford-upon-Avon est connue sous le nom du "pays de Shakespeare" . . . "ce comté que l'on peut appeler le coeur de l'Angleterre". La campagne, les constructions traditionnelles et les racines historiques et littéraires de la région forment une part importante du patrimoine anglais.

On dit que dans le village de **Bidford-on-Avon** Shakespeare aurait eu une sérieuse "gueule de bois" au lendemain d'une fête au pub The Falcon. Ce village est devenu au cours des dernières années la (modeste) Mecque du renouveau de la danse folklorique anglaise appelée "Morris dancing". Les **Shakespeare Morris Men** (Photo page 26) de Stratford-upon-Avon ont soigneusement étudié les danses traditionnelles de Bidford pour les faire renaître. Le "Morris dancing" est un ancien rituel qui remonte à plus de mille ans.

C'est dans la forêt d'Arden, que Shakespeare situa une grande partie de sa pièce As You Like It (Comme il vous plaira). Arden fut également le nom de sa mère. Sur la grande route de Stratford, ne manquez pas le village de **Henley-in-Arden**, parsemé de maisons à colombage penchées (Photo page 26).

Le village de **Baddesley Clinton** doit en partie sa renommée aux méfaits d'un de châtelains: Nicholas Brome, lequel tua le pasteur local parce que ce dernier avait chatouillé sa femme sous le menton.

Cette demeure familiale, Baddesley Clinton Manor (Photo page 27), est un exemple exceptionnel de vieux manoir médiéval entouré de douves.

■ **Chipping Campden's** High Street is considered one of Europe's scenic glories. The name of Chipping Campden refers to its market, and the Market Hall with its arcades and gables in the mellow honey-coloured local stone is a notable example of local building craftsmanship. The church of St James and the almshouses are others. In the 15th century, Chipping Campden was one of the main centres of the Cotswold wool trade and the comfortable houses were built for affluent merchants who settled there. Nearby is Dovers Hill which was where Robert Dover began his Olympic Games in 1612. Unlike the more tame sports of today, Dover's version featured shin-kicking, swordplay and dancing for virgins. The Games came to an end in 1851 after gangs of visiting rowdies disturbed the rural peace.

Broadway has always been the 'big brother' to Chipping Campden. While it has never succeeded in eclipsing the quiet rural charm of its neighbour, it has always preened itself as the more up-market of the two. Broadway has a broad wide street lined with antique and tea shops. The Lygon Arms hotel has been an inn since 1532. Fish Hill, which rises above the town to a height of 300 metres, gives spectacular views across Shakespeare country. At the top, Broadway Tower (*photograph page 28*) stands sentinel.

■ *Die Hauptstraße von **Chipping Campden** gilt als eine der malerischsten Europas. Der Name Chipping Campden bezieht sich eigentlich auf den Markt. Die Markthalle mit Arkaden und Giebeln aus dem honigfarbenen Stein der Gegend ist ein bemerkenswertes Beispiel für die einheimische Baukunst. Architektonisch interessant sind auch die St. James Kirche und das Armenhaus. Im 15. Jahrhundert war Chipping Campden ein wichtiges Zentrum des Wollhandels in den Cotswolds. Die komfortablen Häuser wurden für die reichen Händler gebaut, die sich hier ansiedelten.*

***Broadway** war seit jeher der "große Bruder" von Chipping Campden. Zwar konnte es nie mit dem ruhigen, ländlichen Charm seines Nachbarn konkurrieren, dafür präsentierte es sich immer schon als etwas Vornehmeres. Broadway hat eine breite Hauptstraße mit Antiquitätengeschäften und Teeläden. Das Lygon Arms Hotel ist seit 1532 eine Herberge. Von Fish Hill, 300 Meter über der Stadt, hat man einen großartigen Blick auf das Shakespeare Country. Den Gipfel krönt der Broadway Tower (Foto S. 28).*

■ *La grande rue (High Street) de **Chipping Campden** est considérée comme l'une des splendeurs de l'Europe. Le nom de Chipping Garden fait référence au marché de la ville; les halles, avec leurs arcades et pignons couleur de miel en pierres de la région constituent quant à elles un bon exemple du travail local de construction de bâtiments. Les hospices et l'église de St James en témoignent également. Au XVème siècle, Chipping Campden était un des grands centres du commerce de la laine de Cotswold. Les maisons très confortables alentours furent construites pour les riches marchands venus s'y installer.*

*Le village de **Broadway** a toujours été le "grand frère" de Chipping Campden. S'il n'a jamais réussi à éclipser le paisible charme rural de son voisin, il s'est toujours enorgueilli d'être le marché le mieux approvisionné et le plus achalandé des deux. La rue principale de Broadway est très large et bordée de boutiques d'antiquités et de salons de thé. L'hôtel Lygon Arms accueille les voyageurs depuis 1532. Du haut de Fish Hill, colline de 300 mètres qui surplombe le village, vous aurez une vue magnifique du pays de Shakespeare. Au sommet de la colline, la Broadway Tower (Photo page 28) se dresse telle une sentinelle.*

■ **Warwick**, some eight miles from Stratford, was once a walled town. It boasts a castle described as the 'fairest monument of ancient and chivalrous splendour' whose origins date back a thousand years. It is also the most visited stately home in Britain. Warwick Castle, *(photograph page 29)*, rises 30 metres above the River Avon below it. The castle combines medieval fortress with comfortable mansion, and its attractions range from the State Rooms and Great Hall, *(photograph page 29)* an impressive armoury, dungeon, to haunted towers. The grounds feature a recently recreated Victorian Rose Garden, quiet formal gardens and woodlands and parklands.

■ **Warwick** liegt ca. 13 km von Stratford entfernt und war einst ganz von einer Stadtmauer umgeben. Die Burg, deren Anfänge über tausend Jahre zurückliegen, gilt als das "schönste Denkmal glanzvoller, höfischer Zeiten". Heute sie ist der meistbesuchte alte Adelssitz in Großbritannien. Warwick Castle (Foto S. 29), 30 Meter über dem Avon River, ist eine Kombination aus mittelalterlicher Festung und komfortablem Herrenhaus. Zu den Sehensgürdigkeiten im Inneren gehören die Prunkräume, der große Saal (Foto S. 29), die Waffensammlung, das Verließ und die Türme, in denen es Gespenster geben soll.

■ La ville de Warwick, à quelque douze kilomètres de Stratford, fut autrefois une ville fortifiée. Elle est très fière, encore aujourd'hui, de son château, décrit comme "le plus beau monument reflétant la splendeur de la chevalerie d'autrefois" et dont les origines remontent à plus de mille ans. C'est aussi le château le plus visité de Grande-Bretagne. Le château de Warwick (Photo page 29) surplombe de trente mètres la rivière Avon qui coule à ses pieds. Il présente à la fois l'aspect d'une forteresse médiévale et d'une confortable demeure. On notera en particulier la grande salle de réception et le grand hall (Photo page 29), l'impressionante armurerie, le donjon et les tours hantées.

Roman times. The Tudor buildings in Malt Mill Lane form a picturesque group. Its medieval church and 17th century town hall are also notable examples of the craftsmanship of their respective periods.

These selected villages and towns throughout 'Shakespeare country' each have their own distinct attractions. While they differ from stately graciousness to rustic simplicity, together they form a fascinating backcloth to the focal attraction of the area: the life and times of William Shakespeare.

His appeal, like that of the environment which nurtured and shaped him, is timeless.

"The Indian Empire will go some day, but this Shakespeare... lasts forever with us".
— Thomas Carlyle, 1840.

■ Warwick's **Lord Leycester Hospital** (*photograph page 30*) is considered the finest example of a timber-framed building in the town. In 1571, Robert Dudley, Earl of Leycester, founded his hospital for twelve poor people. It has been run ever since as an almshouse for the aged. The buildings have recently been restored, including the Great Hall of King James, the Guildhall, the Chaplain's Hall and the Brethren's Kitchen.

The fame and name of **Royal Leamington Spa** built up as the town acquired new fashionable features to show off to the world. Leamington refers to the River Leam which flows through it. Spa refers to its 'curative waters', first mentioned in the 16th century but developed in the 18th. (The first spring flowed from a fissure in the rock beside the Parish Church). The grandest part of its name resulted from a visit by Princess Victoria in 1830. When she became Queen she allowed the town to add 'Royal'. The town returned the compliment by calling the bridge over the River Leam the Victoria Bridge.

In its 19th century heyday as a fashionable spa town, the nobility came to drink the waters and to consult Doctor Henry Jephson, who firmly believed in the health-giving powers of the water cures. The elegant Pump Room with its Tuscan colonnade was where the rich and famous gathered.

The Jephson gardens, (*photograph page 30*), named after the physician who helped put the town on the map, form part of Leamington's green heart. They feature a temple, sparkling fountains and an aviary.

Ragley Hall, (*photograph page 31*) family home of the Marquess and Marchioness of Hertford, is a magnificent Palladian mansion set in parkland near Alcester. Designed in 1680 by Robert Hooke, Ragley has a fine collection of paintings, furniture, books and porcelain. It is set in parkland with a lake, an Adventure Wood and country trail.

Alcester itself is a small market town dating back to

■ Das **Lord Leycester Hospital** in Warwick (Foto S. 30) gilt als einer der schönsten Fachwerkbauten der Stadt. Robert Dudley, der Graf von Leycester, gründete es 1571 für zwölf arme Leute. Bis heute wird es als Haus für bedürftige alte Leute benutzt.

Ruf und Ansehen von **Royal Leamington Spa** (Foto S. 30) wuchsen mit dem zunehmenden Angebot für Besucher der Stadt. Der Name Leamington leitet sich vom Fluß Leam ab, der durch die Stadt fließt. Spa bedeutet soviel wie "Kurbad". Die Heilquellen hier werden bereits im 16. Jahrhundert erwähnt, jedoch erst im 18. Jahrhundert genutzt.

Im 19. Jahrhundert erlebte die Stadt ihre Blütezeit als eleganter Badeort vor allem für adelige Kurgäste.

Ragley Hall (Foto S. 31), der Sitz des Marquis von Hertford unweit von Alcester, ist ein prächtiger Palast im Palladio-Stil inmitten einer ausgedehnten Parklandschaft. Der 1680 von Robert Hooke entworfene Bau beherbergt eine ausgezeichnete Gemälde- und Porzellansammlung, hervorragende Möbel und eine großartige Bibliothek. Im Schloßpark finden sich ein See, ein Abenteuerwald und ein Naturlehrpfad.

Alcester selbst ist ein kleiner Marktflecken, der bis auf die Römer zurückgeht. In der Malt Mill Lane steht eine Gruppe malerischer Gebäude im Tudorstil. Weitere interessante Bauwerke sind die mittelalterliche Kirche und das Rathaus aus dem 17. Jahrhundert.

Die Dörfer und Städte im "Shakespeare Country" faszinieren durch ihre vielfältigen Sehenswürdigkeiten, von vornehmen Herrenhäusern bis hin zu malerischen strohgedeckten Cottages. Zusammen bilden sie eine großartige Kulisse für die Hauptattraktion der Gegend: das Leben und die Zeit William Shekespeares.

Seine Anziehungskraft – wie auch die des Landes, das ihn hervorgebracht und formte – ist zeitlos.

"Das indische Imperium wird eines Tages untergehen, Shakespeare . . . bleibt uns für alle Zeit erhalten."
– *Thomas Carlyle, 1840*

■ Le **Lord Leycester Hospital** de Warwick (Photo page 30) constitue le plus bel exemple de construction à structure en bois de la ville. En 1571, Robert Dudley, Comte de Leycester, fonda un hôpital pour douze pauvres. Depuis, cet hôpital a été transformé en maison de retraite.

Royal Leamington Spa, ville d'eau, (Photo page 30) doit sa célébrité à l'attrait qu'elle a su exercer sur le monde extérieur. Le nom de Lemington fait référence à la rivière Leam qui traverse la ville. Le mot "Spa" se rapporte aux bienfaits curatifs de son eau, lesquels furent d'abord soulignés au XVIème siècle mais exploités à partir du XVIIIème.

A l'époque de ses beaux jours, au XIXème siècle, Leamington était devenue une station thermale très à la mode où se rendait la noblesse, qui venait boire sa fameuse eau.

Dressé au milieu d'un parc, près d'Alcester, **Ragley Hall** (Photo page 31) est une magnifique bâtisse de style palladien où vivent le Marquis et la Marquise de Hertford. Construite en 1680 par Robert Hooke, Ragley abrite une splendide collection de tableaux, de meubles, livres et pièces de porcelaine. La demeure est campée au milieu d'un parc où l'on trouve un lac, un "bois aux aventures" et un sentier de promenade.

La petite ville d'**Alcester**, et son marché, remonte elle-même aux temps des Romains. Son groupe de maisons de l'époque des Tudors, dans Malt Mill Lane, est particulièrement pittoresque. Son église médiéval et son hôtel de ville du XVIIème reflètent eux-aussi très bien le type de constructions de leurs époques respectives.

Ces quelques villes et villages du "pays de Shakespeare" présentent tous leurs propres attraits. S'ils se distinguent par leur élégance raffinée ou à l'inverse par leur réelle simplicité rustique, ils forment tous la fascinante toile de fond de l'attraction majeure de la région: la vie et l'époque de William Shakespeare.

L'attrait de cet auteur, comme celui de l'environnement où il fut élevé et qui le façonna, est éternel.

"The Indian Empire will go some day, but this Shakespeare . . . lasts forever with us".
(Un jour nous perdrons l'empire des Indes, mais ce Shakespeare, lui, restera pour toujours avec nous".)
– *Thomas Carlyle, 1840*

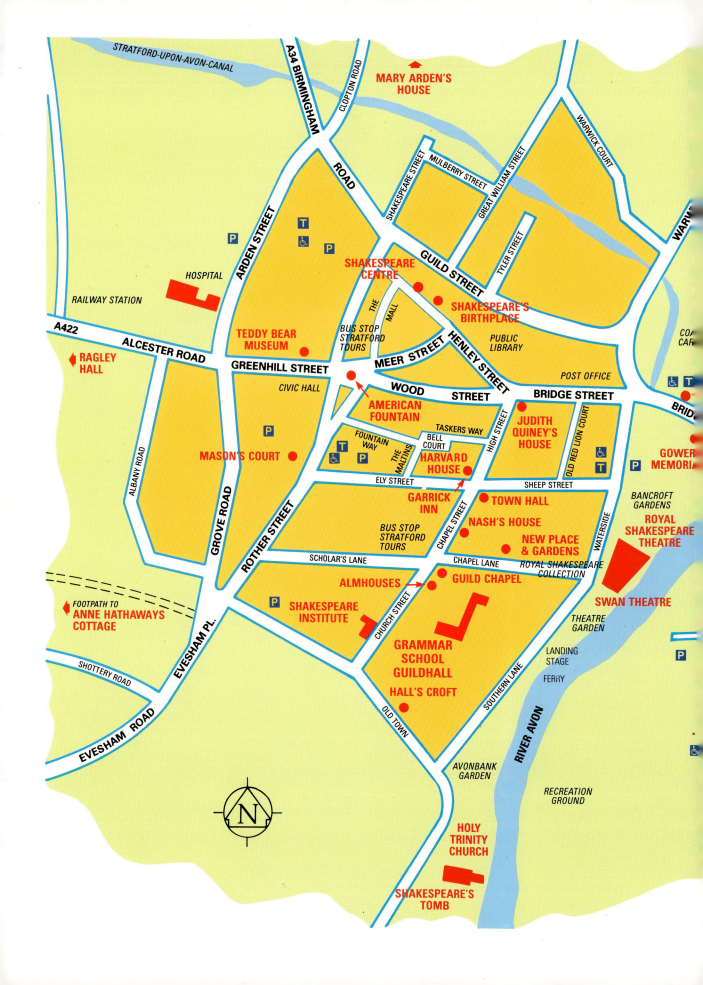